FUNdamental
Science
0 1 2 3 4 5 6 7 8 9 10 11 12 13 14 15 16 17 18 19 20
Key Stage 1

Is It Living or Non-living?

by Ruth Owen

Ruby Tuesday Books

Published in 2016 by Ruby Tuesday Books Ltd.

Editor: Mark J. Sachner
Designer: Emma Randall
Consultant: Judy Wearing, PhD, BEd
Production: John Lingham

Photo credits:
FLPA: 15 (bottom); Getty Images: 29 (top); NASA: 4 (centre), 6 (top), 22; Science Photo Library: 20 (top), 21 (centre), 21 (bottom left); Shutterstock: Cover, 1, 2–3, 4–5, 6 (bottom), 7, 8–9, 10 (bottom), 11 (bottom), 12–13, 14, 15 (top), 16–17, 18–19, 20 (bottom), 21 (top), 21 (bottom right), 23, 24–25, 26–27, 28, 29 (bottom), 30–31; Warren Photographic: 10–11 (top).

British Library Cataloguing in Publication Data (CIP) is available for this title.

ISBN 978-1-910549-81-0

Printed in China by Toppan Leefung

www.rubytuesdaybooks.com

Contents

Words shown in **bold** in the text are explained in the glossary.

The download button shows there are free worksheets or other resources available. Go to:

www.rubytuesdaybooks.com/scienceKS1

Is It Alive or Not Alive?

The world around you is full of many different things.

Some things are alive. Others are not alive.

Sunflower seeds

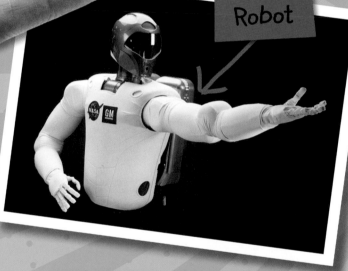

Robot

Football

Plant

Let's Talk

How do you think we can tell if something is alive or not alive?

Worm

Child

Clock

Chick

Milk

Balloon

Let's Investigate!

Look at each of the pictures on pages 4 and 5.

Does the picture show something that's alive or not alive?

Why do you think so?

Draw three boxes in a notebook and give them headings:

Alive	Not alive	Not sure

Sort the pictures by writing the name of each thing in one of the boxes.

(The answers are at the bottom of the page.)

Answer: Alive: child, plant, worm, chick, sunflower seeds. **Not alive:** robot, balloon, clock, football, milk.

5

Question Time

We can discover if something is alive by observing it and asking questions.

Robot

Cat

1   Can it move on its own?

2   Does it need air?

3   Does it need water and food?

4 Does it produce **waste**?

5 Does it react to things that happen around it?

6 Does it grow?

Tree

7 Can it **reproduce**? For example, can it have babies or make new versions of itself?

Let's Talk

Ask these questions about a robot, a cat and a tree.

Do you think these things are alive or not alive?

7

A Cat's Life

Just like all animals big or small, a cat is a living thing. So how do we know a cat is alive?

A cat must breathe to take in **oxygen** to produce **energy**.

A cat must drink water. It also needs to eat food for energy.

A cat reacts to its surroundings in many ways. If you stroke a cat's fur, it reacts by purring. If a cat finds a sunny spot, it reacts by taking a nap.

A cat's body produces waste materials of wee and poo.

These waste materials leave the cat's body to keep the animal healthy.

A cat can move. It runs, plays and can jump five times its own height.

Kitten to Cat

We know that a cat is alive because it grows from a tiny kitten into an adult cat.

Kitten

Once a cat is grown up, it is able to reproduce.

A female cat **mates** with a male cat.
About nine weeks after mating,
she gives birth to her kittens.

Female cat

Kittens drinking milk

Adult cat

Not all animals give birth to their babies.

A hen mates with a cockerel.

Then she lays eggs and sits on them to keep them warm.

After about three weeks, chicks hatch from the eggs.

The little chicks grow up to be hens and cockerels.

Is a Plant Alive?

To find out if a tree or other plant is alive we can ask these questions.

Does a plant need air?

Yes! A plant's leaves take in **carbon dioxide** from air to make energy.

Does a plant need water?

Yes! A plant's roots take in water from soil. They also take in **nutrients** that a plant needs to grow.

Roots

Soil

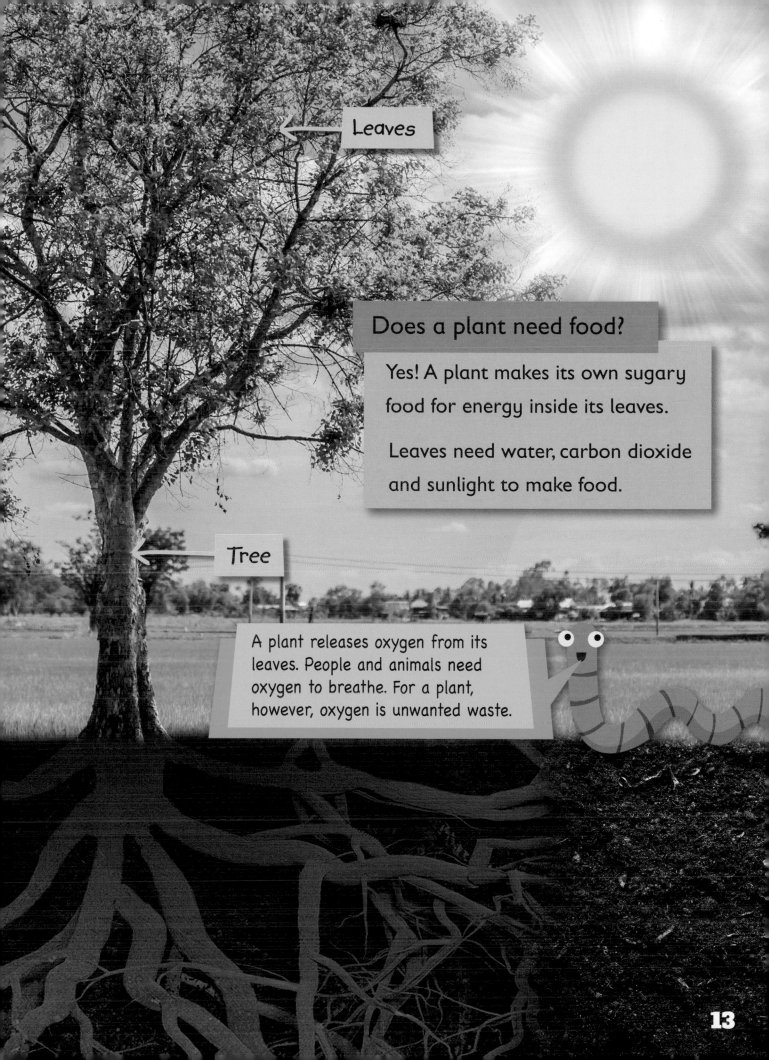

Leaves

Does a plant need food?

Yes! A plant makes its own sugary food for energy inside its leaves.

Leaves need water, carbon dioxide and sunlight to make food.

Tree

A plant releases oxygen from its leaves. People and animals need oxygen to breathe. For a plant, however, oxygen is unwanted waste.

Making New Plants

To discover if plants are alive we can also ask, do they reproduce and grow? The answer is yes!

Most plants reproduce by making seeds.

The seeds of some plants form inside flowers.

Sunflower seeds

Sunflower

Some plants have seeds that form inside fruits.

Fruit

Apple tree seed

A seed is a living thing. It contains all the material needed to grow into a new plant.

A tiny shoot grows from a seed.

The shoot grows and grows to become a plant.

Shoot

Giant bamboo

A type of grass called giant bamboo can grow more than 1 metre in a day!

Let's Talk

Do you think a plant can move and react to its surroundings?

Plants Can Move!

Plants may not be able to run and jump, but they do move!

The leaves of plants need sunlight to make food.

To soak up more sunlight, a plant turns its leaves towards the Sun.

Under the ground, plant roots slowly move and spread through the soil to find water.

Be a Scientist!

Do seedlings move towards sunlight? Let's investigate!

Gather your equipment:
- Empty butter or margarine tub
- Potting compost
- A packet of cress seeds
- A watering can

1. Fill the tub nearly to the top with potting compost.

2. Sprinkle some seeds on top of the soil.

3. Place the tub on a sunny windowsill. Make sure you water the seedlings so the soil doesn't get dry.

Observe the seedlings. Do they grow straight up, towards the window or away from the window?

4. Now turn the tub around so a different side is facing the window.

What do you think the seedlings will do now?

Do seedlings move towards sunlight?

A Speedy Death Trap

There's one type of plant that can react fast!

A Venus flytrap has special leaves called traps.

When an insect steps on a trap it snaps SHUT!

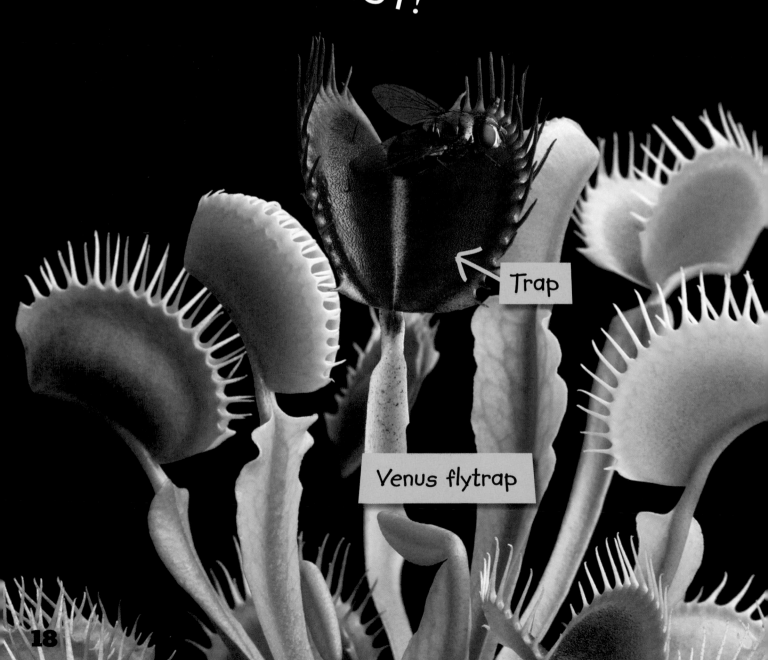

Trap

Venus flytrap

Next the trap oozes juices over its prisoner.

The juices turn all the soft parts of the insect into a soupy mush.

Then the trap soaks up nutrients from the insect soup.

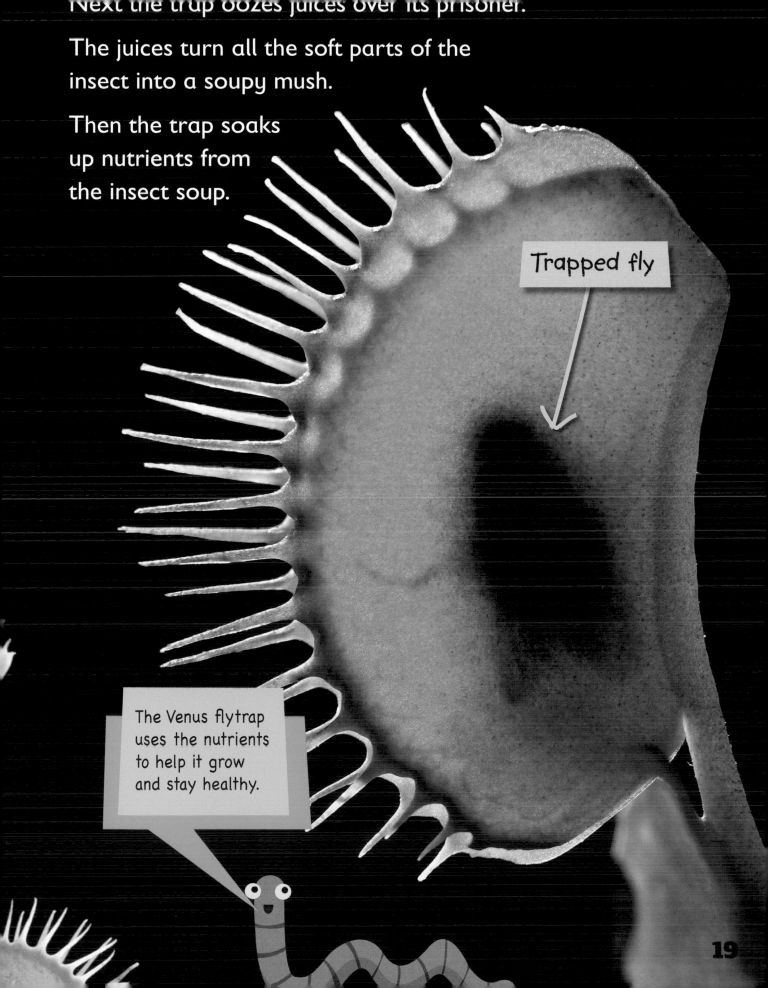

Trapped fly

The Venus flytrap uses the nutrients to help it grow and stay healthy.

Up Close with Living Things

Animals and plants, such as cats and trees, are living things. All living things are made of tiny parts called cells.

Most cells are so small they can only be seen with a very powerful **microscope**.

Cat hair cells

This picture shows the cells that make up a cat's fur. A special microscope zoomed in on the fur to take this picture.

Your body is made of trillions of different cells.

This microscope picture shows human skin cells.

Let's Talk

What special job do the rose petal cells in the picture do?

(The answer is at the bottom of the page.)

Rose petal cells

Answer: The cells are scent cells. They produce a rose's lovely smell.

21

Never Alive!

Did you decide that a robot was alive or not alive? A robot may act as if it's a living thing, but it's not.

A robot doesn't need air, water or food.

It doesn't produce waste and it cannot make robot babies.

A robot can move and react to things around it. It can only do this because people give it instructions.

Robot

Some non-living objects, such as robots, cars and toys, are made by people. These things have never been alive.

Other non-living things, such as clouds, air and water, are found in nature. They have also never been alive.

More Sorting

Some things cannot be sorted as alive or never alive. These things are in a group of their own.

Let's Talk

Look at these four objects. How do you think we could describe them?

Feather

Tomato

Autumn leaf

Log

A leaf, a log, a feather and a tomato are dead.

These objects used to be part of a living thing, but they cannot live on their own.

Tree

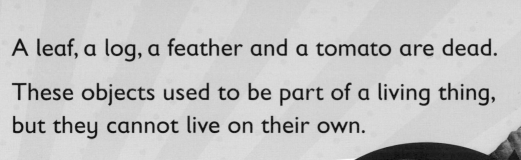

We can describe these things as once alive.

Parrot

Once a tomato is pulled from a plant, it dies. The seeds inside are still alive, though, and can grow into a new plant.

Seeds

Wood in Our World

Many of the objects around us are made of wood.

The wood in all of these objects was once alive.

Trees for wood are grown in huge forests.

Forest →

Tree trunks

The trees are chopped down and cut into planks.

Planks

Then the wood is made into objects in factories and workshops.

It's important to buy wooden objects made from **sustainable** wood. In a sustainable forest new trees are planted to replace the ones that are cut down.

Your Clothes Were Once Alive!

When you wear a cotton T-shirt or jeans, you're wearing something that was once alive!

Cotton comes from cotton plants.

The fluffy, white cotton is harvested from the plants.

Cotton T-shirt

Jeans

At a factory, the cotton is made into fabric on a machine called a loom. Then the fabric is made into clothes.

Loom

Denim

Jeans are made of denim. This tough fabric is made from cotton.

 Let's Explore!

Go on a treasure hunt around your home, garden, classroom or a park.

Can you find or spot the following objects?

- 3 things that are alive
- 3 things that were once alive
- 3 things that have never been alive

29

Alive, Once Alive, Never Alive?

Now it's time to try out everything you've discovered.

Check It Out!

Look at all the objects on these pages.

Are they alive?
Were they once alive?
Or were they never alive?

(The answers are at the bottom of page 31.)

Jellyfish

Corn-on-the-cob

Marker pens

Baby

Bricks

Bird skull

Wool gloves

Pebbles

Pumpkin

Pine cone

Snowflake

Snail

Cactus

Glossary

carbon dioxide
An invisible gas in the air that plants use to make food.

energy
The ability to do work or be active.

mate
To get together to produce young.

microscope
A piece of equipment used for seeing things that are too small to see with your eyes alone.

nutrient
A substance that a living thing needs to grow and be healthy.

oxygen
An invisible gas in air and water that most living things need for survival.

reproduce
To have babies or produce new versions of itself.

sustainable
Something that will not stop but will continue in the future.

waste
Substances that are not needed or wanted by a living thing. Animals produce waste materials of wee and poo.

Index